THE CRUISE JOURNAL

GRAPHIC ARTS CENTER PUBLISHING

International Standard Book Number 1-55868-418-2

© MCMXCVIII by

Graphic Arts Center Publishing Company

P.O. Box 10306 • Portland, Oregon 97296-0306 • 503 / 226-2402

Cartography by Gray Mouse Graphics

Printed and bound in the United States of America

CONTENTS

Welcome to Your Cruise   7

   Cruise Description   9

   The Crew   10

   New Friends & Shipmates   12

   Tablemates   16

   Special Meals   18

   Dazzling Entertainment   20

   Wildlife Sighted   22

   Ports of Call   24

   Planned Shore Excursions   26

   Actual Shore Excursions   30

   Gifts to Purchase   34

   Other Purchases   40

   Photo Notes   42

The Cruise Journal   47

Reference & Future Cruises   135

   Monthly Planning Calendars   136

   Calendars for Four Years   140

   Suggested Supplies   144

   Metric Conversions   146

   Clothing Size Conversions   147

Maps   149

   World Time Zones & Destinations   150

   United States & Canada   152

   Mexico, Central America & the Caribbean   153

   South America & the Panama Canal   154

   Europe & the Baltic   155

   Mediterranean Sea   156

   Africa   157

   Asia   158

   Australia & New Zealand   159

WELCOME
TO YOUR CRUISE

WELCOME

to your cruise aboard the

....

Destination

....

Embarkation date ....

Debarkation date ....

This journal has been created by

....

Cruise Line ....

Stateroom ....

Deck ....

Type of Ship ....

Year Commissioned ....

Ship Specifications ....

....

Port of Embarkation ....

Port of Debarkation ....

Activities on board ....

....

....

....

Other Interesting Facts ....

....

....

....

....

....

....

....

Captain ....

Remarks ....

....

Chief Purser ....

Remarks ....

....

Hotel Manager ....

Remarks ....

....

Cruise Director ....

Remarks ....

....

Maître d'hôtel

Remarks

Dining Room Steward

Remarks

Wine Steward

Remarks

Cabin Steward

Remarks

Name ....

Address ....

....

Phone Number .... e-mail ....

Description ....

....

Name ....

Address ....

....

Phone Number .... e-mail ....

Description ....

....

Name ....

Address ....

....

Phone Number .... e-mail ....

Description ....

....

Name ....

Address ....

....

Phone Number .... e-mail ....

Description ....

....

Name ....

Address ....

....

Phone Number .... e-mail ....

Description ....

....

Name ....

Address ....

....

Phone Number .... e-mail ....

Description ....

....

Name ....

Address ....

....

Phone Number .... e-mail ....

Description ....

....

Name ....

Address ....

....

Phone Number .... e-mail ....

Description ....

....

Name ....

Address ....

....

Phone Number .... e-mail ....

Description ....

....

Name ....

Address ....

....

Phone Number .... e-mail ....

Description ....

....

Name ....

Address ....

....

Phone Number .... e-mail ....

Description ....

....

Name ....

Address ....

....

Phone Number .... e-mail ....

Description ....

....

Name ....

Description ....

....

Name ....

Description ....

....

Name ....

Description ....

....

Name ....

Description ....

....

Name ....

Description ....

....

Name

Description

Name

Description

Name

Description

Name

Description

Name

Description

Date .... Meal ....

Special ....

....

....

Theme ....

Server .... Attire ....

Date .... Meal ....

Special ....

....

....

Theme ....

Server .... Attire ....

Date .... Meal ....

Special ....

....

....

Theme ....

Server .... Attire ....

Date .... Meal ....

Special ....

....

....

Theme ....

Server .... Attire ....

Date .... Meal ....

Special ....

....

....

Theme ....

Server .... Attire ....

Date .... Meal ....

Special ....

....

....

Theme ....

Server .... Attire ....

Date .... Port ....

Location ....

Description ....

....

....

....

Date .... Port ....

Location ....

Description ....

....

....

....

Date .... Port ....

Location ....

Description ....

....

....

....

Date .... Port ....

Location ....

Description ....

....

....

....

Date .... Port ....

Location ....

Description ....

....

....

....

Date .... Port ....

Location ....

Description ....

....

....

....

Date .... Location ....

Description ....

....

Date .... Location ....

Description ....

....

Date .... Location ....

Description ....

....

Date .... Location ....

Description ....

....

Date .... Location ....

Description ....

....

Date .... Location ....

Description ....

....

Date .... Location ....

Description ....

....

Date .... Location ....

Description ....

....

Date .... Location ....

Description ....

....

Date .... Location ....

Description ....

....

Depart / Arrive	Date / Time	Comments

Depart / Arrive	Date / Time	Comments

Port .... Destination ....

....

Address ....

....

Notes ....

....

Port .... Destination ....

....

Address ....

....

Notes ....

....

Port .... Destination ....

....

Address ....

....

Notes ....

....

Port .... Destination ....

....

Address ....

....

Notes ....

....

Port .... Destination ....

....

Address ....

....

Notes ....

....

Port .... Destination ....

....

Address ....

....

Notes ....

....

Port .... Destination ....

....

Address ....

....

Notes ....

....

Port .... Destination ....

....

Address ....

....

Notes ....

....

Port .... Destination ....

....

Address ....

....

Notes ....

....

Port .... Destination ....

....

Address ....

....

Notes ....

....

Port .... Destination ....

....

Address ....

....

Notes ....

....

Port .... Destination ....

....

Address ....

....

Notes ....

....

Date .... Port ....

Location ....

Memories ....

....

....

....

Date .... Port ....

Location ....

Memories ....

....

....

....

Date .... Port ....

Location ....

Memories ....

....

....

....

Date .... Port ....

Location ....

Memories ....

....

....

....

Date .... Port ....

Location ....

Memories ....

....

....

....

Date .... Port ....

Location ....

Memories ....

....

....

....

Date .... Port ....

Location ....

Memories ....

....

....

....

Date .... Port ....

Location ....

Memories ....

....

....

....

Date .... Port ....

Location ....

Memories ....

....

....

....

Date .... Port ....

Location ....

Memories ....

....

....

....

Date .... Port ....

Location ....

Memories ....

....

....

....

Date .... Port ....

Location ....

Memories ....

....

....

....

Name ....

Address ....

....

Phone number ....

Gift idea .... Size, etc. ....

Item purchased .... Date ....

Amount paid .... Currency ....

Payment method .... Place purchased ....

Ship date .... Ship method ....

Name ....

Address ....

....

Phone number ....

Gift idea .... Size, etc. ....

Item purchased .... Date ....

Amount paid .... Currency ....

Payment method .... Place purchased ....

Ship date .... Ship method ....

Name ....

Address ....

....

Phone number ....

Gift idea .... Size, etc. ....

Item purchased .... Date ....

Amount paid .... Currency ....

Payment method .... Place purchased ....

Ship date .... Ship method ....

Name ....

Address ....

....

Phone number ....

Gift idea .... Size, etc. ....

Item purchased .... Date ....

Amount paid .... Currency ....

Payment method .... Place purchased ....

Ship date .... Ship method ....

Name ....

Address ....

....

Phone number ....

Gift idea .... Size, etc. ....

Item purchased .... Date ....

Amount paid .... Currency ....

Payment method .... Place purchased ....

Ship date .... Ship method ....

Name ....

Address ....

....

Phone number ....

Gift idea .... Size, etc. ....

Item purchased .... Date ....

Amount paid .... Currency ....

Payment method .... Place purchased ....

Ship date .... Ship method ....

Name ....

Address ....

....

Phone number ....

Gift idea .... Size, etc. ....

Item purchased .... Date ....

Amount paid .... Currency ....

Payment method .... Place purchased ....

Ship date .... Ship method ....

Name ....

Address ....

....

Phone number ....

Gift idea .... Size, etc. ....

Item purchased .... Date ....

Amount paid .... Currency ....

Payment method .... Place purchased ....

Ship date .... Ship method ....

Name ....

Address ....

....

Phone number ....

Gift idea .... Size, etc. ....

Item purchased .... Date ....

Amount paid .... Currency ....

Payment method .... Place purchased ....

Ship date .... Ship method ....

Name ....

Address ....

....

Phone number ....

Gift idea .... Size, etc. ....

Item purchased .... Date ....

Amount paid .... Currency ....

Payment method .... Place purchased ....

Ship date .... Ship method ....

Name ....

Address ....

....

Phone number ....

Gift idea .... Size, etc. ....

Item purchased .... Date ....

Amount paid .... Currency ....

Payment method .... Place purchased ....

Ship date .... Ship method ....

Name ....

Address ....

....

Phone number ....

Gift idea .... Size, etc. ....

Item purchased .... Date ....

Amount paid .... Currency ....

Payment method .... Place purchased ....

Ship date .... Ship method ....

Item purchased .... Date ....

Amount paid .... Currency ....

Method .... Intended recipient ....

Place purchased ....

Item purchased .... Date ....

Amount paid .... Currency ....

Method .... Intended recipient ....

Place purchased ....

Item purchased .... Date ....

Amount paid .... Currency ....

Method .... Intended recipient ....

Place purchased ....

Item purchased .... Date ....

Amount paid .... Currency ....

Method .... Intended recipient ....

Place purchased ....

Item purchased .... Date ....

Amount paid .... Currency ....

Method .... Intended recipient ....

Place purchased ....

Item purchased .... Date ....

Amount paid .... Currency ....

Method .... Intended recipient ....

Place purchased ....

Item purchased .... Date ....

Amount paid .... Currency ....

Method .... Intended recipient ....

Place purchased ....

Item purchased .... Date ....

Amount paid .... Currency ....

Method .... Intended recipient ....

Place purchased ....

Roll # .... Dates from .... to ....

Locations ....

....

Roll # .... Dates from .... to ....

Locations ....

....

Roll # .... Dates from .... to ....

Locations ....

....

Roll # .... Dates from .... to ....

Locations ....

....

Roll # .... Dates from .... to ....

Locations ....

....

Roll # .... Dates from .... to ....

Locations ....

....

Roll # .... Dates from .... to ....

Locations ....

....

Roll # .... Dates from .... to ....

Locations ....

....

Roll # .... Dates from .... to ....

Locations ....

....

Roll # .... Dates from .... to ....

Locations ....

....

Roll # .... Dates from .... to ....

Locations ....

....

Roll # .... Dates from .... to ....

Locations ....

....

Roll # .... Dates from .... to ....

Locations ....

....

Roll # .... Dates from .... to ....

Locations ....

....

Roll # .... Dates from .... to ....

Locations ....

....

Roll # .... Dates from .... to ....

Locations ....

....

Roll # .... Dates from .... to ....

Locations ....

....

Roll # .... Dates from .... to ....

Locations ....

....

Roll # .... Dates from .... to ....

Locations ....

....

Roll # .... Dates from .... to ....

Locations ....

....

Roll # .... Dates from .... to ....

Locations ....

....

Roll # .... Dates from .... to ....

Locations ....

....

Roll # .... Dates from .... to ....

Locations ....

....

Roll # .... Dates from .... to ....

Locations ....

....

Roll # .... Dates from .... to ....

Locations ....

....

THE CRUISE

JOURNAL

REFERENCE &
FUTURE CRUISES

Month .... *Year*						
SUNDAY	MONDAY	TUESDAY	WEDNESDAY	THURSDAY	FRIDAY	SATURDAY

			Month .... *Year*			
SUNDAY	MONDAY	TUESDAY	WEDNESDAY	THURSDAY	FRIDAY	SATURDAY

Month				*Year*		
SUNDAY	MONDAY	TUESDAY	WEDNESDAY	THURSDAY	FRIDAY	SATURDAY

Month				*Year*		
SUNDAY	MONDAY	TUESDAY	WEDNESDAY	THURSDAY	FRIDAY	SATURDAY

JANUARY

S	M	T	W	T	F	S
				1	2	3
4	5	6	7	8	9	10
11	12	13	14	15	16	17
18	19	20	21	22	23	24
25	26	27	28	29	30	31

FEBRUARY

S	M	T	W	T	F	S
1	2	3	4	5	6	7
8	9	10	11	12	13	14
15	16	17	18	19	20	21
22	23	24	25	26	27	28

MARCH

S	M	T	W	T	F	S
1	2	3	4	5	6	7
8	9	10	11	12	13	14
15	16	17	18	19	20	21
22	23	24	25	26	27	28
29	30	31				

APRIL

S	M	T	W	T	F	S
			1	2	3	4
5	6	7	8	9	10	11
12	13	14	15	16	17	18
19	20	21	22	23	24	25
26	27	28	29	30		

MAY

S	M	T	W	T	F	S
					1	2
3	4	5	6	7	8	9
10	11	12	13	14	15	16
17	18	19	20	21	22	23
24	25	26	27	28	29	30
31						

JUNE

S	M	T	W	T	F	S
	1	2	3	4	5	6
7	8	9	10	11	12	13
14	15	16	17	18	19	20
21	22	23	24	25	26	27
28	29	30				

JULY

S	M	T	W	T	F	S
			1	2	3	4
5	6	7	8	9	10	11
12	13	14	15	16	17	18
19	20	21	22	23	24	25
26	27	28	29	30	31	

AUGUST

S	M	T	W	T	F	S
						1
2	3	4	5	6	7	8
9	10	11	12	13	14	15
16	17	18	19	20	21	22
23	24	25	26	27	28	29
30	31					

SEPTEMBER

S	M	T	W	T	F	S
		1	2	3	4	5
6	7	8	9	10	11	12
13	14	15	16	17	18	19
20	21	22	23	24	25	26
27	28	29	30			

OCTOBER

S	M	T	W	T	F	S
				1	2	3
4	5	6	7	8	9	10
11	12	13	14	15	16	17
18	19	20	21	22	23	24
25	26	27	28	29	30	31

NOVEMBER

S	M	T	W	T	F	S
1	2	3	4	5	6	7
8	9	10	11	12	13	14
15	16	17	18	19	20	21
22	23	24	25	26	27	28
29	30					

DECEMBER

S	M	T	W	T	F	S
		1	2	3	4	5
6	7	8	9	10	11	12
13	14	15	16	17	18	19
20	21	22	23	24	25	26
27	28	29	30	31		

JANUARY

S	M	T	W	T	F	S
					1	2
3	4	5	6	7	8	9
10	11	12	13	14	15	16
17	18	19	20	21	22	23
24	25	26	27	28	29	30
31						

FEBRUARY

S	M	T	W	T	F	S
	1	2	3	4	5	6
7	8	9	10	11	12	13
14	15	16	17	18	19	20
21	22	23	24	25	26	27
28						

MARCH

S	M	T	W	T	F	S
	1	2	3	4	5	6
7	8	9	10	11	12	13
14	15	16	17	18	19	20
21	22	23	24	25	26	27
28	29	30	31			

APRIL

S	M	T	W	T	F	S
				1	2	3
4	5	6	7	8	9	10
11	12	13	14	15	16	17
18	19	20	21	22	23	24
25	26	27	28	29	30	

MAY

S	M	T	W	T	F	S
						1
2	3	4	5	6	7	8
9	10	11	12	13	14	15
16	17	18	19	20	21	22
23	24	25	26	27	28	29
30	31					

JUNE

S	M	T	W	T	F	S
		1	2	3	4	5
6	7	8	9	10	11	12
13	14	15	16	17	18	19
20	21	22	23	24	25	26
27	28	29	30			

JULY

S	M	T	W	T	F	S
				1	2	3
4	5	6	7	8	9	10
11	12	13	14	15	16	17
18	19	20	21	22	23	24
25	26	27	28	29	30	31

AUGUST

S	M	T	W	T	F	S
1	2	3	4	5	6	7
8	9	10	11	12	13	14
15	16	17	18	19	20	21
22	23	24	25	26	27	28
29	30	31				

SEPTEMBER

S	M	T	W	T	F	S
			1	2	3	4
5	6	7	8	9	10	11
12	13	14	15	16	17	18
19	20	21	22	23	24	25
26	27	28	29	30		

OCTOBER

S	M	T	W	T	F	S
					1	2
3	4	5	6	7	8	9
10	11	12	13	14	15	16
17	18	19	20	21	22	23
24	25	26	27	28	29	30
31						

NOVEMBER

S	M	T	W	T	F	S
	1	2	3	4	5	6
7	8	9	10	11	12	13
14	15	16	17	18	19	20
21	22	23	24	25	26	27
28	29	30				

DECEMBER

S	M	T	W	T	F	S
			1	2	3	4
5	6	7	8	9	10	11
12	13	14	15	16	17	18
19	20	21	22	23	24	25
26	27	28	29	30	31	

JANUARY

S	M	T	W	T	F	S
						1
2	3	4	5	6	7	8
9	10	11	12	13	14	15
16	17	18	19	20	21	22
23	24	25	26	27	28	29
30	31					

FEBRUARY

S	M	T	W	T	F	S
		1	2	3	4	5
6	7	8	9	10	11	12
13	14	15	16	17	18	19
20	21	22	23	24	25	26
27	28	29				

MARCH

S	M	T	W	T	F	S
			1	2	3	4
5	6	7	8	9	10	11
12	13	14	15	16	17	18
19	20	21	22	23	24	25
26	27	28	29	30	31	

APRIL

S	M	T	W	T	F	S
						1
2	3	4	5	6	7	8
9	10	11	12	13	14	15
16	17	18	19	20	21	22
23	24	25	26	27	28	29
30						

MAY

S	M	T	W	T	F	S
	1	2	3	4	5	6
7	8	9	10	11	12	13
14	15	16	17	18	19	20
21	22	23	24	25	26	27
28	29	30	31			

JUNE

S	M	T	W	T	F	S
				1	2	3
4	5	6	7	8	9	10
11	12	13	14	15	16	17
18	19	20	21	22	23	24
25	26	27	28	29	30	

JULY

S	M	T	W	T	F	S
						1
2	3	4	5	6	7	8
9	10	11	12	13	14	15
16	17	18	19	20	21	22
23	24	25	26	27	28	29
30	31					

AUGUST

S	M	T	W	T	F	S
		1	2	3	4	5
6	7	8	9	10	11	12
13	14	15	16	17	18	19
20	21	22	23	24	25	26
27	28	29	30	31		

SEPTEMBER

S	M	T	W	T	F	S
					1	2
3	4	5	6	7	8	9
10	11	12	13	14	15	16
17	18	19	20	21	22	23
24	25	26	27	28	29	30

OCTOBER

S	M	T	W	T	F	S
1	2	3	4	5	6	7
8	9	10	11	12	13	14
15	16	17	18	19	20	21
22	23	24	25	26	27	28
29	30	31				

NOVEMBER

S	M	T	W	T	F	S
		1	2	3	4	
5	6	7	8	9	10	11
12	13	14	15	16	17	18
19	20	21	22	23	24	25
26	27	28	29	30		

DECEMBER

S	M	T	W	T	F	S
					1	2
3	4	5	6	7	8	9
10	11	12	13	14	15	16
17	18	19	20	21	22	23
24	25	26	27	28	29	30
31						

JANUARY

S	M	T	W	T	F	S
	1	2	3	4	5	6
7	8	9	10	11	12	13
14	15	16	17	18	19	20
21	22	23	24	25	26	27
28	29	30	31			

FEBRUARY

S	M	T	W	T	F	S
				1	2	3
4	5	6	7	8	9	10
11	12	13	14	15	16	17
18	19	20	21	22	23	24
25	26	27	28			

MARCH

S	M	T	W	T	F	S
				1	2	3
4	5	6	7	8	9	10
11	12	13	14	15	16	17
18	19	20	21	22	23	24
25	26	27	28	29	30	31

APRIL

S	M	T	W	T	F	S
1	2	3	4	5	6	7
8	9	10	11	12	13	14
15	16	17	18	19	20	21
22	23	24	25	26	27	28
29	30					

MAY

S	M	T	W	T	F	S
		1	2	3	4	5
6	7	8	9	10	11	12
13	14	15	16	17	18	19
20	21	22	23	24	25	26
27	28	29	30	31		

JUNE

S	M	T	W	T	F	S
					1	2
3	4	5	6	7	8	9
10	11	12	13	14	15	16
17	18	19	20	21	22	23
24	25	26	27	28	29	30

JULY

S	M	T	W	T	F	S
1	2	3	4	5	6	7
8	9	10	11	12	13	14
15	16	17	18	19	20	21
22	23	24	25	26	27	28
29	30	31				

AUGUST

S	M	T	W	T	F	S
			1	2	3	4
5	6	7	8	9	10	11
12	13	14	15	16	17	18
19	20	21	22	23	24	25
26	27	28	29	30	31	

SEPTEMBER

S	M	T	W	T	F	S
						1
2	3	4	5	6	7	8
9	10	11	12	13	14	15
16	17	18	19	20	21	22
23	24	25	26	27	28	29
30						

OCTOBER

S	M	T	W	T	F	S
	1	2	3	4	5	6
7	8	9	10	11	12	13
14	15	16	17	18	19	20
21	22	23	24	25	26	27
28	29	30	31			

NOVEMBER

S	M	T	W	T	F	S
				1	2	3
4	5	6	7	8	9	10
11	12	13	14	15	16	17
18	19	20	21	22	23	24
25	26	27	28	29	30	

DECEMBER

S	M	T	W	T	F	S
						1
2	3	4	5	6	7	8
9	10	11	12	13	14	15
16	17	18	19	20	21	22
23	24	25	26	27	28	29
30	31					

Health & First Aid Supplies

❑ ❑ ❑ Prescription drugs

❑ ❑ ❑ Vitamins

❑ ❑ ❑ Antihistimine

❑ ❑ ❑ Calamine lotion

❑ ❑ ❑ Diarrhea medication

❑ ❑ ❑ Salve for cuts / bug bites

❑ ❑ ❑ Indigestion remedy

❑ ❑ ❑ Insect repellent

❑ ❑ ❑ Laxative

❑ ❑ ❑ Lip balm

❑ ❑ ❑ Motion-sickness remedy

❑ ❑ ❑ Petroleum jelly

❑ ❑ ❑ Band-aids / bandages

❑ ❑ ❑ Ace bandages

❑ ❑ ❑ Birth control / condoms

❑ ❑ ❑ Headache / pain medication

❑ ❑ ❑ Antacid medication

Personal Needs

❑ ❑ ❑ Contact lenses / solution

❑ ❑ ❑ Glasses

❑ ❑ ❑ Toothbrush / toothpaste

❑ ❑ ❑ Dental floss

❑ ❑ ❑ Deodorant

❑ ❑ ❑ Feminine hygiene

❑ ❑ ❑ Comb / brush

❑ ❑ ❑ Shampoo / conditioner

❑ ❑ ❑ Shower cap

❑ ❑ ❑ Hair dryer / curler

❑ ❑ ❑ Skin lotion

❑ ❑ ❑ Sunblock

❑ ❑ ❑ Laundry soap

❑ ❑ ❑ Perfume / aftershave

❑ ❑ ❑ Towel / washcloth

❑ ❑ ❑ Make-up

❑ ❑ ❑ Nail care supplies

✓ boxes as follows:

❑ ❑ ❑ Need to purchase / Laid out / Packed

Documents

- ❏ ❏ ❏ Birth certificate / ID
- ❏ ❏ ❏ Driver's license
- ❏ ❏ ❏ Health insurance
- ❏ ❏ ❏ Insurance policy
- ❏ ❏ ❏ Passport / visas
- ❏ ❏ ❏ Travel documents / tickets
- ❏ ❏ ❏ Telephone calling card
- ❏ ❏ ❏ Traveler's checks
- ❏ ❏ ❏ Credit cards

Outdoor & Weather-related Items

- ❏ ❏ ❏ Flashlight
- ❏ ❏ ❏ Raincoat / umbrella
- ❏ ❏ ❏ Sun hat / visor
- ❏ ❏ ❏ Sunglasses
- ❏ ❏ ❏ Swimsuit / goggles
- ❏ ❏ ❏ Bathing cap
- ❏ ❏ ❏ Thongs / deck sandals
- ❏ ❏ ❏ Sweater / jacket
- ❏ ❏ ❏ Walking shoes

Stationery

- ❏ ❏ ❏ Address book
- ❏ ❏ ❏ Business cards
- ❏ ❏ ❏ Playing cards
- ❏ ❏ ❏ Small notebook
- ❏ ❏ ❏ Sketch pad
- ❏ ❏ ❏ Stationery / stamps

Assorted Sundries

- ❏ ❏ ❏ Adapter / converter
- ❏ ❏ ❏ Binoculars / ear plugs
- ❏ ❏ ❏ Calculator
- ❏ ❏ ❏ Camera / film / batteries
- ❏ ❏ ❏ Video camera / tapes
- ❏ ❏ ❏ Pocket knife
- ❏ ❏ ❏ Knapsack / carryall bag
- ❏ ❏ ❏ Money belt
- ❏ ❏ ❏ Portable radio / batteries
- ❏ ❏ ❏ Spot remover / mending kit
- ❏ ❏ ❏ Travel iron
- ❏ ❏ ❏ Travel clock

Unit	Abbreviation	Approximate US Equivalent
LENGTH		
kilometer	km	0.62 mile
hectometer	hm	328.08 feet
dekameter	dam	32.81 feet
meter	m	39.37 inches
decimeter	dm	3.94 inches
centimeter	cm	0.39 inch
millimeter	mm	0.039 inch
AREA		
square kilometer	sq km *or* km	0.3861 square mile
hectare	ha	2.47 acres
are	a	119.60 square yards
square centimeter	sq cm *or* cm²	0.155 square inch
VOLUME		
cubic meter	m³	1.307 cubic yards
cubic decimeter	dm³	61.023 cubic inches
cubic centimeter	cu cm *or* cm³ *or* cc	0.061 cubic inch
CAPACITY		
kiloliter	kl	1.31 cubic yards
hectoliter	hl	3.53 cubic feet
decaliter	dal	2.64 gallons
liter	l	1.057 quarts
deciliter	dl	0.21 pint
centiliter	cl	0.338 fluid ounce
milliliter	ml	0.27 fluid dram
MASS & WEIGHT		
metric ton	t	1.102 short tons
kilogram	kg	2.2046 pounds
hectogram	hg	3.527 ounces
dekagram	dag	0.353 ounce
gram	g	0.035 ounce

CELSIUS, CENTIGRADE, & FAHRENHEIT
Celsius or Centigrade times 2 approximates Fahrenheit temperatures.
Water boils at 100° Celsius and freezes at 0° C.
Water boils at 212° Fahrenheit and freezes at 32° F.

LADIES

Dress, suit, coat, & sweater sizes

Canada / US	8	10	12	14	16	18
UK	10	12	14	16	18	20
Cont. Europe	38	40	42	44	46	48
Australia	10	12	14	16	18	20

Shoes

Canada / US	5	5½	6	6½	7	7½	8	8½	9	9½	10
UK	3½	4	4½	5	5½	6	6½	7	7½	8	8½
Cont. Europe	35	36	36	37	37	38	38	39	39	40	40
France	35	35	36	37	38	38	39	39	40	41	42
Australia	5	5½	6	6½	7	7½	8	8½	9	9½	10

GENTLEMEN

Suit, jacket, & sweater sizes

Canada / US / UK	34	35	36	37	38	39	40	41	42
Cont. Europe	44	46	48	49½	51	52½	54	55½	57
Australia	12	14		16		18		20	

Shirts

Canada / US / UK	14½	15	15½	16	16½	17	17½	18
Cont. Europe	37	38	39	41	42	43	44	45
Australia	37	38	39	41	42	43	44	45

Shoes

Canada / US	7	8	9	10	11	12	13
UK	6	7	8	9	10	11	12
Cont. Europe	40	41	42	43	44½	46	47
Australia	6	7	8	9	10	11	12

MAPS

Argentina, Buenos Aires	+ 2		Netherlands, Amsterdam	+ 6
Australia, Adelaide	+ 14		New Guinea, Port Moresby	+ 15
Australia, Sydney	+ 15		New Zealand, Auckland	+ 17
Bahamas, Nassau	EST		Nigeria, Lagos	+ 6
Belgium, Brussels	+ 6		Norway, Oslo	+ 6
Bermuda	+ 1		Panama	EST
Brazil, Rio de Janeiro	+ 2		Peru, Lima	EST
Cambodia, Phnom Penh	+ 12		Philippines, Manila	+ 13
Canada, Prince Edward Is.	+ 1		Portugal, Lisbon	+ 5
Canada, St. John's, NF	+ 1½		Puerto Rico, San Juan	+ 1
Canada, Vancouver, BC	- 3		Russian Fed., St. Petersburg	+ 8
Chile, Santiago	+ 1		Saudi Arabia, Riyadh	+ 8
China, Hong Kong	+ 13		Singapore	+ 13
Colombia, Bogotá	EST		South Africa, Cape Town	+ 7
Cuba, Havana	EST		Spain, Barcelona	+ 6
Denmark, Copenhagen	+ 6		Sri Lanka, Colombo	+ 10½
Egypt, Cairo	+ 7		Sweden, Stockholm	+ 6
France, Marseilles	+ 6		Switzerland, Berne	+ 6
Germany, Berlin	+ 6		Tahiti	- 5
Greece, Athens	+ 7		Taiwan, Kaohsung	+ 13
Haiti, Port-au-Prince	EST		Thailand, Bangkok	+ 12
India, Bombay	+ 10½		United Kingdom, London	+ 5
Indonesia, Jakarta	+ 12		USA, Alaska, Anchorage	- 4
Israel, Haifa	+ 7		USA, Alaska, Glacier Bay	- 4
Italy, Rome	+ 6		USA, Alaska, Valdez	- 4
Jamaica, Kingston	EST		USA, California, San Francisco	- 3
Japan, Tokyo	+ 14		USA, Florida, Miami	EST
Korea, Rep. of, Seoul	+ 14		USA, Hawaii, Honolulu	- 5
Malaysia, Kuala Lumpur	+ 13		USA, Louisiana, New Orleans	- 1
Mexico, Acapulco	- 1		USA, Massachusetts, Boston	EST
Mexico, Veracruz	- 1		USA, New York, New York	EST
Monaco	+ 6		Venezuela, Caracas	+ 1

Time is plus or minus Eastern Standard Time (EST).

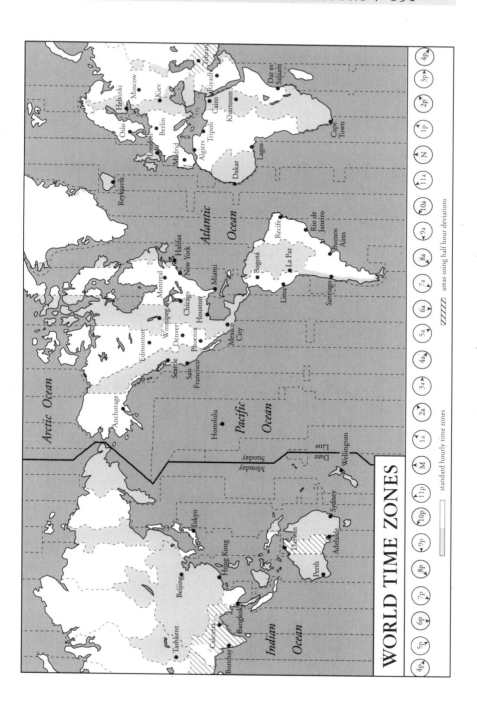

WORLD TIME ZONES

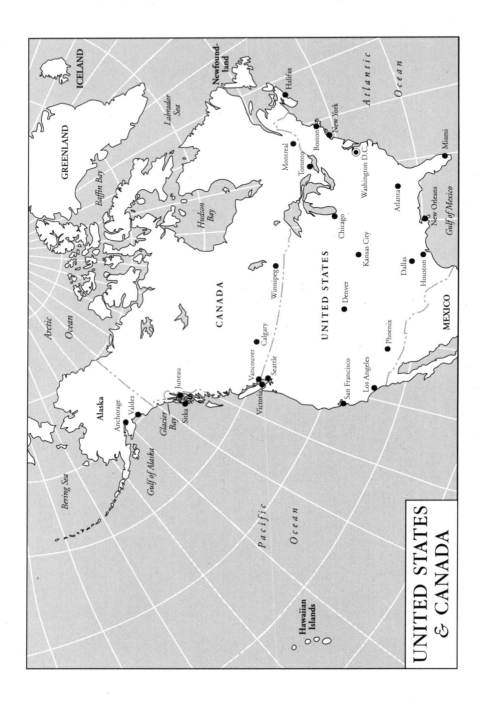

UNITED STATES
& CANADA

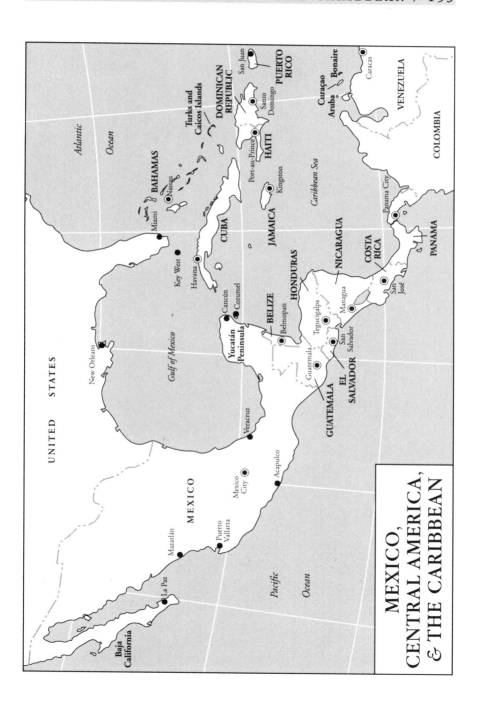

MEXICO, CENTRAL AMERICA, & THE CARIBBEAN

Caribbean Sea

Guadeloupe
Dominica
Martinique
St. Lucia
St. Vincent
Barbados
Grenada
Tobago
Trinidad

Panama Canal Panama City

Caracas

PANAMA

Gulf of Panama

VENEZUELA

Georgetown
Paramaribo
Cayenne

Atlantic

Bogotá

COLOMBIA

FRENCH GUIANA

Quito

GUYANA

ECUADOR

SURINAME

PERU

Lima

BRAZIL

Salvador

La Paz

Brasilia

BOLIVIA

Rio de Janeiro

PARAGUAY

São Paulo

Asunción

Ocean

ARGENTINA

Pacific

Santiago

Buenos Aires
Montevideo

CHILE

URUGUAY

Ocean

SOUTH AMERICA & THE PANAMA CANAL

Falkland Islands

Strait of Magellan

Tierra del Fuego

Cape Horn

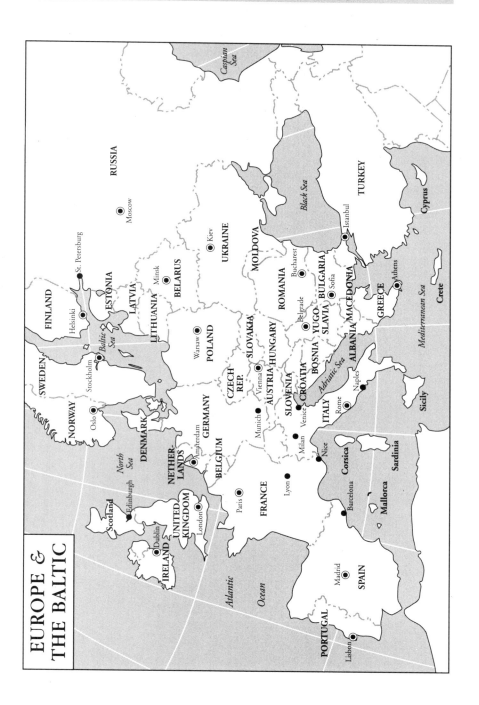

EUROPE &
THE BALTIC

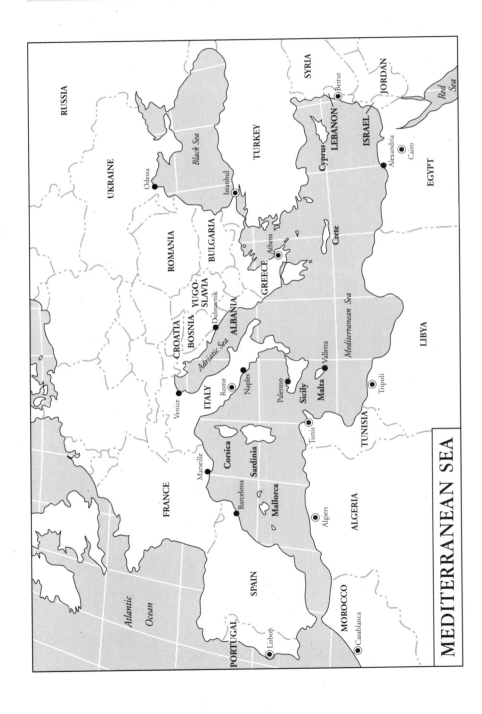

MEDITERRANEAN SEA

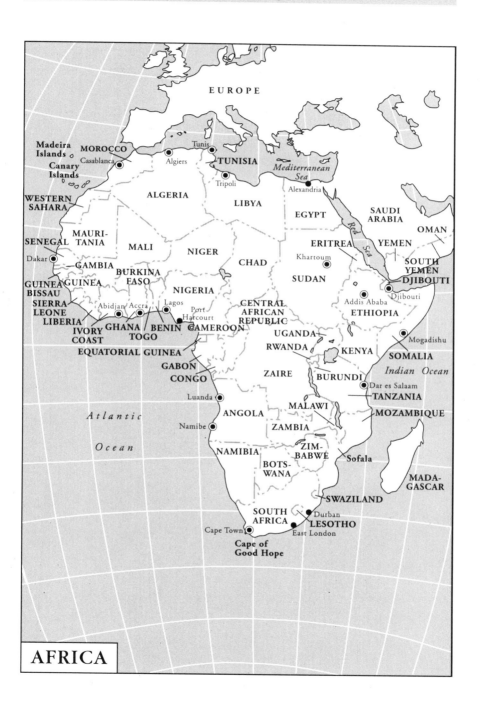

EUROPE

Madeira
Islands
MOROCCO
Canary
Islands

Tunis
TUNISIA
Algiers
Casablanca
Tripoli

WESTERN
SAHARA

ALGERIA

LIBYA

Mediterranean
Sea
Alexandria

EGYPT

SAUDI
ARABIA

OMAN

MAURI-
TANIA
SENEGAL

MALI

NIGER

CHAD

ERITREA

Red Sea

YEMEN

SOUTH
YEMEN

Dakar
GAMBIA
GUINEA-
BISSAU
GUINEA
BURKINA
FASO

Khartoum

SUDAN

DJIBOUTI
Djibouti

SIERRA
LEONE
LIBERIA
Abidjan
Accra
Lagos

NIGERIA

CENTRAL
AFRICAN
REPUBLIC

Addis Ababa
ETHIOPIA

IVORY
COAST
GHANA
BENIN
TOGO
CAMEROON
Port
Harcourt

UGANDA
RWANDA

KENYA

Mogadishu

EQUATORIAL GUINEA

GABON
CONGO

ZAIRE

BURUNDI

SOMALIA

Indian Ocean

Luanda

Dar es Salaam
TANZANIA

Atlantic

ANGOLA

MALAWI

MOZAMBIQUE

Namibe

ZAMBIA

Ocean

NAMIBIA

ZIM-
BABWE

Sofala

BOTS-
WANA

MADA-
GASCAR

SWAZILAND

SOUTH
AFRICA
Cape Town
Durban
LESOTHO
East London

Cape of
Good Hope

AFRICA

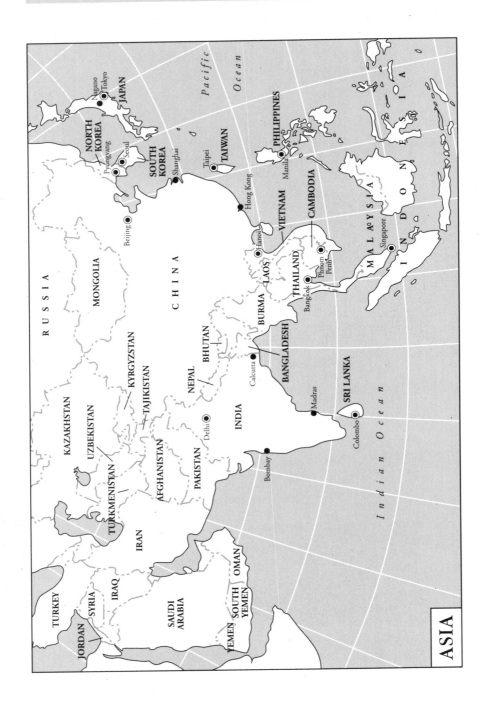

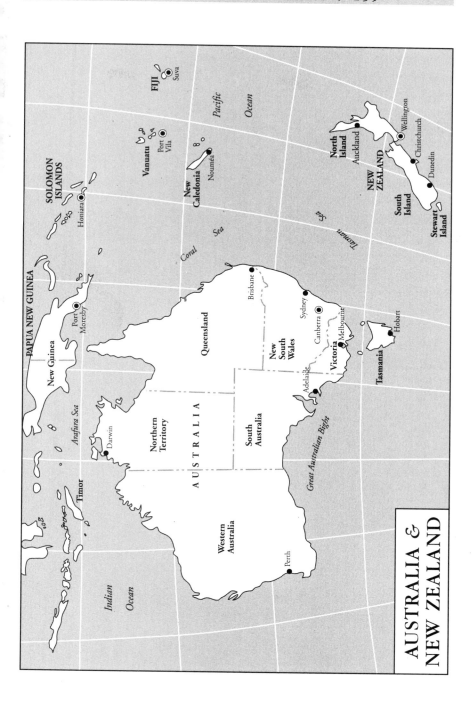

AUSTRALIA &
NEW ZEALAND